HEART
OF
GOLD

LITTLE ACTS OF KINDNESS

Robie Rogge and Dian G. Smith

Clarkson Potter/Publishers
New York

Copyright © 2020 by ROBIE LLC

All rights reserved.

Published in the United States by Clarkson Potter/Publishers, an
imprint of Random House, a division of Penguin Random House
LLC, New York.
clarksonpotter.com

CLARKSON POTTER is a trademark and POTTER with colophon
is a registered trademark of Penguin Random House LLC.

ISBN 978-1-5247-6232-2

Printed in China

CONCEIVED AND COMPILED BY
Robie Rogge and Dian G. Smith

BOOK AND COVER DESIGN
Jessie Kaye

10 9 8 7 6 5 4 3 2 1

First Edition

> Words are mere bubbles of water,
> but deeds are drops of gold.

—TIBETAN PROVERB

Most of us sincerely intend to do kind deeds, but these intentions, like bubbles, are too often fragile and short-lived. Time passes, obligations interfere, memory fades. *Heart of Gold* will help you to transform your good intentions into concrete acts of kindness.

This unique book offers specific suggestions for helping people you know and don't know, as well as the larger community. Flip through the pages for something that resonates in your heart today. Do that kind act or one in the same spirit and check it off by placing a gold heart sticker in the outline at the bottom of the page. Deed by deed and page by page, you will be filling the book and also filling your own heart.

Apologize for a mistake or a slight.

THANK SOMEONE
FOR A KINDNESS.

Reconnect with an old friend.

Invite a new colleague for coffee.

Volunteer at a local shelter.

COLLECT FOOD FOR A FOOD PANTRY.

♥

Smile at people on the street.

♥

Compliment a stranger.

Plant flowers
or trees in your
community park or
a window box for
passersby to see.

CARRY A PLASTIC BAG
TO PICK UP LITTER
ON YOUR BLOCK.

Take someone
to a doctor's
appointment.

Visit someone in the hospital.

♥

Cheer for kids
on a local team.

♠

BECOME A BIG BROTHER OR SISTER.

VIDEO-CALL YOUR PARENTS, GRANDPARENTS, OR A RELATIVE YOU RARELY SEE.

Send a care package to a soldier overseas.

Help someone who doesn't speak English.

GIVE DIRECTIONS TO SOMEONE WHO LOOKS LOST.

❤

Take a shelter dog for a walk.

♠

Donate needed supplies to an animal shelter.

Volunteer at a local political office.

LISTEN RESPECTFULLY TO SOMEONE WITH DIFFERENT POLITICAL VIEWS.

OFFER COMPUTER HELP TO A SENIOR CITIZEN OR ANYONE WHO WANTS TO LEARN.

Volunteer at a school or an after-school program.

Welcome new neighbors and introduce them to others.

ORGANIZE A BLOCK PARTY.

GROCERY SHOP OR
DO ANOTHER ERRAND
FOR AN ELDERLY
OR FRAIL PERSON.

Babysit, do laundry, or cook for new parents.

Pay for the person behind you in line at a coffee shop.

PUT COINS IN AN EXPIRED PARKING METER.

♥

Bring cookies or flowers to the office.

♠

Bring cookies or flowers to a fire or police station.

Rake the leaves on your block.

SHOVEL THE SNOW FROM A NEIGHBOR'S STEPS.

♥

Organize a
fund-raiser for
a cause.

♥

Donate your coffee money to a charity.

Give up your seat on the bus or train.

LEAVE BEHIND
YOUR NEWSPAPER
OR MAGAZINE FOR
OTHERS TO READ.

♥

Share your umbrella in a downpour.

♠

Share produce or flowers from your garden or from a farmers' market.

Donate or recycle old electronics.

DONATE BOOKS
TO A LIBRARY.

Compliment a parent whose child is well-behaved in a restaurant.

Relay an overheard compliment.

Bring a meal to someone who is sick.

READ TO SOMEONE WHO IS SICK OR BLIND.

Donate blood or encourage others to.

Learn CPR.

Give a homemade gift.

OFFER YOUR HOME
REPAIR SKILLS TO
SOMEONE.

♥

Register as an organ donor.

Register as a bone marrow donor.

Be a designated driver or offer to pay for a taxi.

DRIVE OR TAKE SOMEONE TO VOTE.

♥

Collect school supplies for children in shelters.

♠

Collect gifts for needy children during the holidays.

Celebrate an "un-birthday."

THROW SOMEONE
A SURPRISE PARTY.

♥

Speak up when
someone is
bullied.

♠

Short-circuit gossip.

Work in a community garden.

SUPPORT FARMERS AT A LOCAL GREENMARKET.

♥

Sponsor a child overseas.

♥

"Adopt" an endangered animal.

Make
a match.

TALK TO A PERSON WHO SEEMS SHY AT A PARTY.

♥

Participate in a race or walk for a cause.

♠

Give water to people running or walking for a charity.

Write to a boss praising a helpful employee.

WRITE A NOTE ON THE
RESTAURANT CHECK
AND LEAVE A BIG TIP
FOR GOOD SERVICE.

❤

Leave out seeds for birds in the winter.

♠

Volunteer at a local nature conservancy.

Invite someone lonely to a holiday dinner.

INVITE SOMEONE
LONELY TO A
CONCERT OR PLAY.

Put away your
phone when
you are with
someone.

Resist multitasking during a conversation.

Buy a meal for a homeless person.

DONATE TO AN
ORGANIZATION THAT
SERVES THE HOMELESS.

♥

Volunteer at a nursing home.

♠

Visit someone living in a nursing home.

Help people register to vote.

CONTACT AN ELECTED OFFICIAL ABOUT A CAUSE YOU BELIEVE IN.

Surprise your partner with a "What I ♥ Most About You" list.

Put sticky notes with affirmations on the mirrors in restrooms.

Comfort a friend in distress.

GIVE A FRIEND A
BOOK YOU LOVE.

Mentor a young person or a newcomer to your field.

Make a helpful business introduction.

Volunteer for a hotline.

MAKE FUND-RAISING CALLS FOR A CAUSE YOU SUPPORT.

❤

Thank your
parents.

♠

Write to a former teacher or other professional who made a difference in your life.

Reach out to someone in trouble.

PROTEST AN INJUSTICE.

CARE FOR THE PET
AND PLANTS OF A
FRIEND WHO IS AWAY.

Collect mail for a friend who is away.

Be kind to a customer service agent.

ANSWER YOUR PHONE IN A WELCOMING VOICE.

♥

Visit a home-bound friend.

♥

Take a walk with a friend recovering from an illness.

Let a car merge into your lane.

SMILE OR WAVE TO
THE PERSON WHO
LETS YOU MERGE INTO
A TRAFFIC LANE.

Give helpful tips
to someone new
to this country.

Offer to take a photo for a group of tourists.

Give an encouraging hug.

TEXT SOMEONE JUST
TO SAY GOOD MORNING
OR GOOD NIGHT.

♥

Praise someone on social media.

♠

Donate to a friend's cause online or off-line.

Contribute to a local newsletter.

IF YOU SEE SOMETHING, SAY SOMETHING.

USE A REUSABLE SHOPPING BAG, COFFEE MUG, AND WATER BOTTLE.

Each time you get a new piece of clothing, give an old one away.

Give little gifts to your friends on *your* birthday.

SEND A LETTER IN THE
MAIL TO A FRIEND
INSTEAD OF A TEXT.

❤

Read to kids in the library for story time.

♠

Hide a dollar bill or a happy note in a library book.

Surprise a family member with breakfast in bed.

MAKE YOUR FAMILY
OR FRIENDS HOT
CHOCOLATE ON A
COLD DAY.

♥

Bike or walk
rather than drive.

♥

Carpool or take public transportation.

Let someone in a hurry get ahead of you in line.

HELP SOMEONE
CARRY HEAVY BAGS.

Leave a quarter in a gumball machine, vending machine, or washing machine for the next person.

Leave a thank-you note on the windshield of a car that has a veteran sticker.

Eat in restaurants that donate leftover food to soup kitchens or food pantries.

URGE RESTAURANTS TO DONATE THEIR EXTRA FOOD TO THE HUNGRY.

♥

Do a chore your partner hates.

♥

Bring in a neighbor's trash cans.

Buy parking passes for parents of children in the hospital.

VOLUNTEER AS A GREETER AT A HOSPITAL.

♥

Donate prepaid phone cards to a shelter.

♥

Donate toiletries to a shelter.

Help a friend move and unpack.

GIVE COUPONS
FROM A LOCAL ICE
CREAM SHOP AS A
HOUSEWARMING GIFT.

DONATE MONEY, FOOD,
OR TIME TO A PLACE
EXPERIENCING A
NATURAL DISASTER.

Promote causes that concern you on social media.

Help someone economize by reviewing subscriptions and services.

HELP SOMEONE SORT AND STORE ONLINE PHOTOS.

♥

Offer an extra bedroom to a visitor.

♠

Offer the use of your car to someone who needs it.

Encourage someone else to volunteer.